I0554911

Introduction

This is a workbook. It includes 28 daily prompts based on the plot structure of Jane Austen's Pride and Prejudice.

There are 6 (and a bit) blank journal pages for each day which should give you enough space to write the 1786 words per day that will get you to the 50,000 word goal by the end of 4 weeks.

Each day includes:

   a short description of the action/plot point from Pride and Prejudice

   a To Do item (the goal of the day)

   a description of the scene to write

Do not revise/edit as you write – the goal is to get the writing down on the page, not to perfect it (yet).

A Writer's Workbook / Journal

28 Days of Guided Writing Prompts

(How to Journal 50,000 Words in a Month)

© Suzan Digh 2023

ISBN: 978-1-998061-13-6

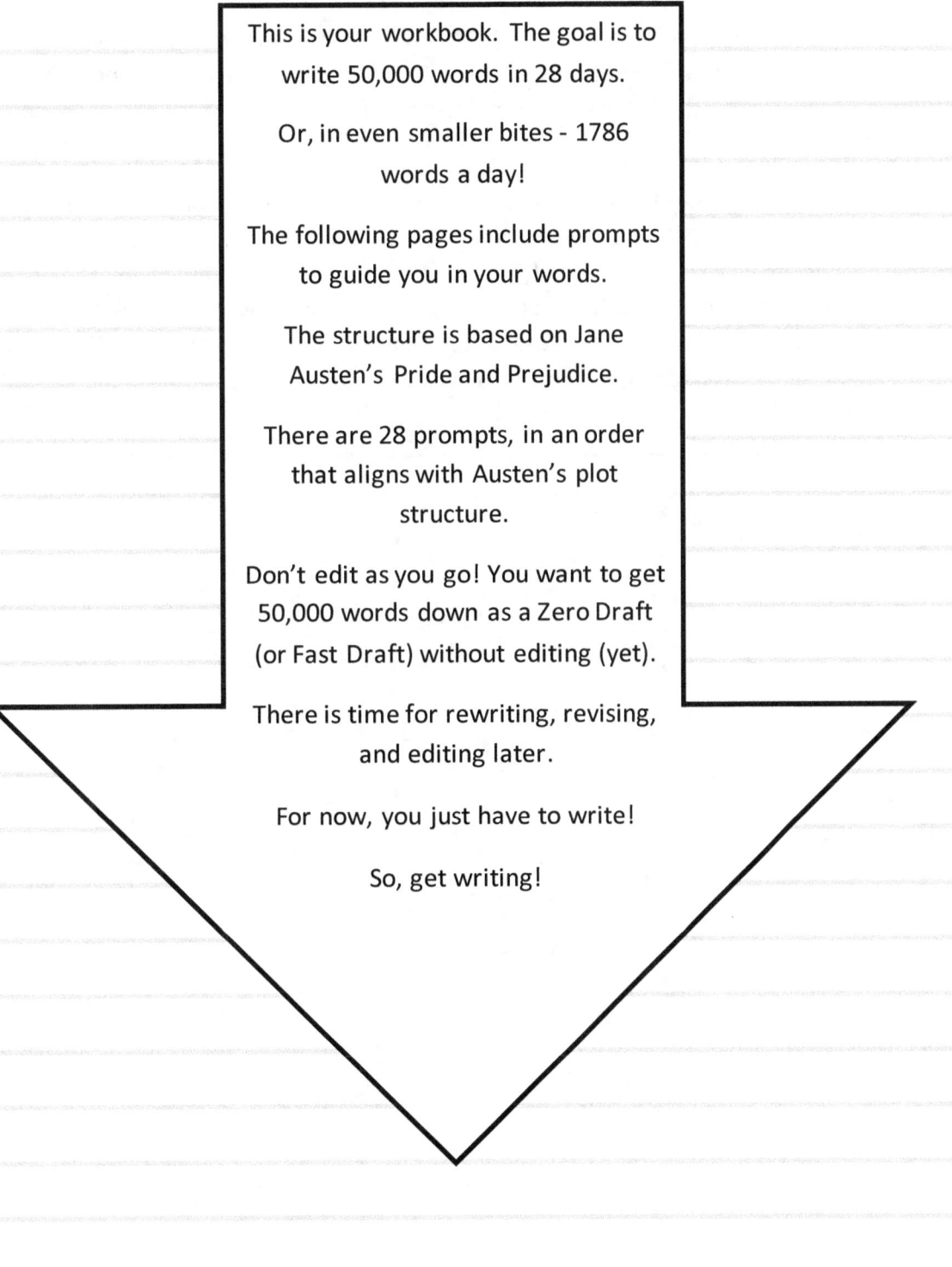

This is your workbook. The goal is to write 50,000 words in 28 days.

Or, in even smaller bites - 1786 words a day!

The following pages include prompts to guide you in your words.

The structure is based on Jane Austen's Pride and Prejudice.

There are 28 prompts, in an order that aligns with Austen's plot structure.

Don't edit as you go! You want to get 50,000 words down as a Zero Draft (or Fast Draft) without editing (yet).

There is time for rewriting, revising, and editing later.

For now, you just have to write!

So, get writing!

Day 1

Austen: Introduces the Bennet family and the arrival of Mr. Bingley, a wealthy bachelor.

To Do: Introduce the main character (MC). Who is she, where is she, who does she live with. Who are her family. How old is she. Does she live with family, spouse, alone, roommates? Is she in school, college, unemployed, professional job, a welder? Does she have a dream?

The Scene: Write a scene where we see the main character for the first time. What is she doing? Where is she at? Who is there with her? Why did she go there? What does she expect to happen while she is there? At the end of the scene, is she happy? Sad? Frustrated? Angry? What made her feel that way? End the scene with something that makes the reader want to read the next chapter: did her dress get torn as she fled? Did she see a love interest kissing someone else? Did her sibling get shot dead at the podium during a speech?

Day 2

Austen: Mrs. Bennet attempts to arrange a marriage between Mr. Bingley and one of her daughters. She isn't concerned about *which* daughter though, just any one of them.

To Do: Develop a character/situation that creates a pressure for the MC to connect with a romantic interest. This could be parental pressure to marry, loneliness and tired of being alone, a recent breakup and a rebound situation. We want the MC to be exposed to the opportunity to meet someone.

The Scene: Write a scene where the MC is questioning whether or not she wants to meet someone. Perhaps write about a previous relationship and how it ended badly, or how she is heart broken after catching her ex cheating. We want the MC to "go out" to meet the romantic interest but having some background/history on her will shade how the initial meeting will impact her.

Day 3

Austen: Mr. Bingley hosts a ball, and Elizabeth meets Mr. Darcy, who comes across as rude and arrogant.

To Do: Identify the first romantic interest [Mr. Bingley]. This won't be "The Love", but it will be someone that "might" be of interest. Introduce the True Love [Mr. Darcy] but have the MC not be at all interested.

The Scene: Write about where they meet - is it a ball? A bar? A friend's house? Work? Who else is there? Who introduces MC to [Mr. Bingley], what is [Mr. Bingley] like? What is his background? Write about his last relationship and who it was with and how it ended and how he feels about that old relationship. Is he looking for love?

Introduce [Mr. Darcy], but he is just "in passing". MC can form some quick opinion of him. Did he bump into her and spill her drink and not replace it? Did he steal her cab? Did he pinch her bottom at the office?

Day 4

Austen: Mr. Bingley and Mr. Darcy leave Netherfield, much to the dismay of the Bennet family.

To Do: Identify why the love interests [Mr. Bingley] and [Mr. Darcy] are leaving. Investigate why the MC is dismayed over this departure.

The Scene: Write the "goodbye" scene (the scene where the MC is jolted into actions that create the reason for the change that people will read this book for) - did the lover slip out in the night without a goodbye, how did the MC find out he was leaving? Did she overhear a conversation, or did he tell her directly, how did that conversation go? Did [Mr. Darcy] play a role in the decision to leave? Did he insist the MC was not "good enough" for his friend and MC overheard?

Is MC really upset? How do we know? What does she do? Cry? Call her mother? Hit him? Steal and drive off in his car?

Day 5

Austen: Jane, the eldest Bennet daughter, falls ill and is forced to stay at Netherfield.

To Do: Start a subplot. This will "draw off" the love interest [Mr. Bingley] a few scenes later so set up the situation that will enable [Mr. Bingley] to be "taken away from" the MC.

The Scene: Introduce this [sickly eldest daughter]. This can be a past lover returned, a dream job in a different city, a sick relative (even the MC's sister, if you want). Identify where this [sickly daughter] is, how she/it is attractive to [Mr. Bingley] (explore why he would give up the MC for her/it).

Day 6

Austen: Elizabeth walks to Netherfield to visit Jane and encounters Mr. Darcy, who is surprised by her presence.

To Do: Have the MC cross paths with the main love interest [Mr. Darcy] while she is trying to hold onto the departing love interest by trying to get involved with the thing that he is leaving her for (so, if [Mr. Bingley] left MC for a job in a new city, MC could go to that city, or tell him she is willing to move there with him).

The Scene: The goal is to a) show that the MC *thinks* she wants to hold on to [Mr. Bingley] while b) forcing her to run into and interact with [Mr. Darcy], in such a way that there is a spark of some kind. Perhaps she goes to Bingley's office to tell him she will move with him, and Darcy catches her in the stairwell and tells her she has no business pressuring [Mr. Bingley].

Day 7

Austen: Elizabeth and Mr. Darcy argue, and she begins to develop a negative opinion of him.

To Do: Create a detailed interaction that explores both the MC and [Mr. Darcy's] opposing points of view.

The Scene: They get into a heated argument about — her following Bingley around, her job, her ex-lover, her lofty attitude, etc. Flesh out his point of view as well: why is he opposing her? Has he had trouble communicating with women before? Does he see her as a shrew? Or a victim and he is trying to "protect her"? Why is he dismissive? How does their argument unfold? What does MC think of his behavior? How does he express his opinion of her behaviour to his friend [Mr. Bingley]?

Day 8

Austen: Jane recovers and returns home, while Elizabeth visits Charlotte Lucas, a friend who is soon to be married.

To Do: Next step in the subplot (started on Day 5).

The Scene: Whatever it was that lured [Mr. Bingley] away from the MC has become even more attractive (and will certainly pull the love interest permanently away from the MC). What is this thing, why is it so attractive, what about it has lured [Mr. Bingley]? (Has he finally been offered his dream job? Has he fallen head over heels in love when he has spent his life thinking he never would love again?)

Introduce a secondary "foil" for the MC - this is likely her best friend, sister, confident, gay high school buddy, etc. This person will eventually "rescue" the MC from ending up with the wrong person [Mr. Collins].

Day 9

Austen: Mr. Collins, a distant cousin of the Bennet family, arrives and proposes to Elizabeth, who declines.

To Do: Create the "thing the MC does not want". This will be the antithesis of the MC's dreams and goals. This is who the "foil" was created for in Day 8.

The Scene: The antithesis [Mr. Collins] arrives unexpectedly. An arranged marriage partner? A blind date? Someone from high school? A former lover who has returned to the country after 2 years posted overseas? As the scene progresses, show the MC's growing unease - is she shifting in her seat, trying to escape, sneaking to the bathroom to call her own landline for an excuse to leave? Use dialogue and actions to create tension and enhance the discomfort.

Day 10

Austen: Mr. Collins proposes to Charlotte Lucas, who accepts.

To Do: Bring the foil (from day 8) and the antithesis (from day 9) together.

The Scene: We already know the MC does not want this [Mr. Collins]. This scene could start with some hesitance from the MC ("am I making the right decision by kicking this guy out?") or it can be full relief ("thank goodness Cynthia was looking for Mr. Right and he has the money to support her while she recovers from her treatments").

The MC should be central to bringing these two together - perhaps it was an intervention, or she called her friend to come over right away because she knew [Mr. Collins] was going to show up and she wanted an excuse as to why he can't stay to visit. We want to retain a connection between the MC and one or both of these characters because on Day 11 we use this relationship to bring the main plot thread forward.

Day 11

Austen: Elizabeth visits her friend, Mr. and Mrs. Collins, and meets Mr. Darcy's aunt, Lady Catherine de Bourgh.

To Do: Bring the MC to visit the foil (her friend from Day 8) and/or [Mr. Collins] from day 9 in such as way as to make it possible to both "run into" the main love interest next (Day 12) and enable a situation where the MC will find another reason why that main love interest won't work (Day 15).

The Scene: Because these relationships were developed separately but they were also brought together in Day 10, this scene can be a follow-up from Day 10 where the MC goes, for example, to the new couple's elopement party where the MC watches the new couple and wishes she could have that, or is grateful that she dodged getting hooked up with [Mr. Collins], or, she decides she will be single forever because it only leads to infidelities (explore a past experience with this, perhaps).

Day 12

Austen: Mr. Darcy unexpectedly arrives at Rosings Park, Lady Catherine's estate, and continues to behave arrogantly towards Elizabeth.

To Do: Have the MC run into [Mr. Darcy] and they have an awkward or unpleasant encounter.

The Scene: The foil and [Mr. Collins] made it possible for the MC to be at a place or in a situation where she now has to interact with [Mr. Darcy]. Write this scene so that she is (pleasantly or unpleasantly) surprised to see him here. He is not "attractive" to her at this time - perhaps she sees him with another woman at a party, or he is obscenely drunk, or he gets into a fist fight, or she thinks he has been spreading rumors that they "hooked up" previously, etc.

Day 13

Austen: Mr. Darcy reveals his true feelings for Elizabeth, and she is shocked.

To Do: Shed light on [Mr. Darcy's] behavior (i.e., from Day 12) and have him subtly express interest in the MC.

The Scene: Show how [Mr. Darcy's] earlier behavior was just how he coped with his feelings for the MC - perhaps he, like her, did not want a relationship. Maybe he is part of a very rich family, and she is not, and his family wouldn't like her. Maybe [Mr. Collins] had told him that the MC was actually a money-seeking socialite, and this is why he had been acting so poorly/mean/dismissive. He will express that he really likes her, but in such a way that she doesn't believe him (i.e., she thinks he is drunk, or he only wants to sleep with her).

Day 14

Austen: Elizabeth reflects on her feelings towards Mr. Darcy.

To Do: Explore the MC's feeling for [Mr. Darcy]. There should be some attraction mixed in with her dislike - we are hoping to get to "I don't *want* to want him, but I do" type thinking.

The Scene: After she rejects [Mr. Darcy], explore what she is thinking about - she must realize that she is interested/attracted/intrigued, at least enough that she cares when she is further criticized about her "value" (Day 15). Perhaps via a conversation with her best friend (the foil), after the party goers disperse and [Mr. Collins] is passed out in the other room. Create some more back-story as to why [Mr. Darcy] would be aloof, or undesirable. Or why the MC would think *she* is undesirable.

Day 15

Austen: Lady Catherine de Bourgh interrogates Elizabeth about her family and her upbringing.

To Do: Have an outsider support the MC's belief that she (the MC) is not "worthy" of [Mr. Darcy]. Have the MC interact with the "bad guy" [Mr. Wickham].

The Scene: Someone the MC doesn't know very well but who is important to [Mr. Darcy] (maybe his mother, his best friend, etc.) reflects the MC's own concerns back on the MC. If the MC thinks that she isn't good enough for [Mr. Darcy] because she is scarred, or poor, or has a child from an early relationship, this person will reinforce that.

We also need to introduce [Mr. Wickham] - perhaps he seduces the MC because she is looking for a distraction from how she feels about [Mr. Darcy]. Or perhaps he encourages her to invest in his business or provide his buy-in to a high stakes poker game and he claims he will share the winnings.

Day 16

Austen: Mr. Darcy proposes to Elizabeth, but she rejects him, citing his treatment of Mr. Wickham, a family friend.

To Do: Take it a step farther than on Day 13 where [Mr. Darcy] hinted at being interested - now the interest is more than fleeting.

The Scene: The situation has to be such that [Mr. Darcy] expresses his feelings in such a way that the *reader* knows he means it, but, at the same time, he denigrates the relationship the MC has with [Mr. Wickham] (from Day 15) which puts the MC's hackles up because she has some sort of deal going with [Mr. Wickham] and thinks the "bad-mouthing" is unjustified or spiteful.

Day 17

Austen: Elizabeth receives a letter from Mr. Darcy explaining his actions towards Mr. Wickham.

To Do: Have [Mr. Darcy] "come clean" as to his relationship with [Mr. Wickham] (or, *nearly* come clean).

The Scene: [Mr. Darcy] realizes he has feelings for the MC, and he must come clean about his involvement with [Mr. Wickham] so that he is not "hiding" anything from her. This conversation might not (and probably should not) put [Mr. Darcy] in a good light. The reader wants it to be honest, but we don't want to resolve the tension just yet, so he can't come out of it looking fully innocent. Perhaps they ran a scam together back when they were in university, or perhaps [Mr. Darcy] had covered up for a crime [Mr. Wickham] had committed.

Day 18

Austen: The Bennet family travels to visit Mr. Collins' father, where Elizabeth meets Mr. Wickham again and learns more about his past with Mr. Darcy.

To Do: The MC meets with [Mr. Wickham] and now she knows he has had a less-than-honorable past. She confronts him.

The Scene: The MC is apprehensive because she wants to trust [Mr. Wickham]. She doesn't want to be taken for a fool, nor does she really want to admit that [Mr. Darcy] was trying to protect her. She has feelings for [Mr. Darcy] but still wants to deny these feelings. Every bad thing about [Mr. Darcy] that "resolves" makes it harder for her to deny her feelings.

Why does she want to deny these feelings? Because the last time (Day 4) she thought she loved someone [Mr. Bingley], she was wrong, and the other possibilities for love that she has been exposed to are negative: [Mr. Collins] and [Mr. Wickham].

Day 19

Austen: The Bennet family returns home, and Mr. Bingley returns to Netherfield and invites Jane to a ball.

To Do: Carry on the [Mr. Bingley] subplot (started in #5, continued in #8). Help the MC resolve her feelings about love.

The Scene: Show a healthy relationship [Mr. Bingley]; make sure the MC sees this relationship as healthy and desirable. Expand the relationship with [Mr. Wickham]. Perhaps the MC can explore the "gossip" she had heard about him but make it so that the MC can't resolve the conflict or "clear the air" (we will use Day 25 for that). Perhaps have [Mr. Wickham] provide a plausible explanation, or, better, have a "friend" such as [Mr. Collins or the foil] support [Mr. Wickham] (innocently - because they don't know the truth of [Mr. Wickham], or maliciously if that fits with your story tone).

Day 20

Austen: Mr. Bingley proposes to Jane, and she accepts.

To Do: Close the [Mr. Bingley] subplot (started in #5, continued in #8 and #19) You will be returning to this thread at the very end of the book, to show full closure and that the MC is "okay" with this resolution.

The Scene: The MC acknowledges that love doesn't always turn out wrong; there is happily ever after. Dangle this in front of the MC so that she can almost see herself finding a similar love (i.e., with [Mr. Darcy]). Have her figure out/explore what it is that will make her as happy as these two are.

Day 21

Austen: Elizabeth visits her friend, Charlotte, who has married Mr. Collins, and observes the unpleasant dynamics of their marriage.

To Do: Demonstrate that the MC sees the relationship between her friend (the foil) and Mr. Collins as unhappy (and not something she herself would want). This is the opposite reaction to how she feels about the relationship/situation with [Mr. Bingley].

The Scene: The MC is exposed to some sort of conflict between [Mr. Collins] and the foil. Perhaps they are fighting (physically or otherwise), and the MC has to call the police, or the MC witnesses [Mr. Collins] doing something inappropriate such as kissing another woman or pickpocketing from the coats at the coat check at a fund-raising event where he is volunteering because the foil insisted he must volunteer to help at the charity event.

Day 22

Austen: Mr. Darcy and Mr. Bingley visit the Bennet family, and Mr. Darcy behaves kindly towards them. Elizabeth is impressed by his changed behavior.

To Do: Fresh from seeing how unpleasant the relationship is between [Mr. Collins] and the foil, she becomes more interested in [Mr. Darcy] because he is not at all like [Mr. Collins].

The Scene: Bring the MC and [Mr. Darcy] together in a situation where they are not one-on-one. The MC cannot directly interact with [Mr. Darcy] in a way that would allow them to resolve their conflict (that comes just a little bit later), but it should show [Mr. Darcy] in a good light. Perhaps they are out at a social event and the MC is offended (or assaulted) by a very drunk [Mr. Collins] or [Mr. Wickham] and [Mr. Darcy] steps up to defend her (honor) in front of the partygoers before escorting the "bad guy" out of the room.

Day 23

Austen: Lydia, the youngest Bennet daughter, runs away with Mr. Wickham.

To Do: [Mr. Wickham] breaks the trust of the MC. His actions are despicable, and they devastate the MC.

The Scene: This is where the true nature of [Mr. Wickham] becomes clear to the MC, and his bad behavior very negatively impacts the MC. This could be that [Mr. Wickham] committed a crime, and when he was arrested, accused the MC of being an accomplice, or he used his relationship with the MC to gain access to her father's home, where he stole a valuable item. This scene should be devastating to the MC and must involve very high stakes - her hopes and dreams should be dashed.

Day 24

Austen: Mr. Darcy helps locate Lydia and Mr. Wickham and arranges for them to marry.

To Do: [Mr. Darcy] comes to the rescue. But the MC does not know this yet!

The Scene: [Mr. Darcy] saves the MC. She cannot know who saved her, yet, as that is what is exposed in Day 25. So, whatever evil thing [Mr. Wickham] did on Day 23, the blame is removed from the MC today. For example, if [Mr. Wickham] had been arrested for a crime and claimed that the MC was his accomplice and she was subsequently arrested and is now sitting in an interrogation room, this would be the scene where the police let her go, but don't explain why (which is because [Mr. Darcy], unknown to the MC, provided information that absolved the MC).

Day 25

Austen: Mr. Collins visits Longbourn and informs the family of Mr. Darcy's involvement in Lydia's scandal.

To Do: The antithesis (the exact thing the MC does not want) is the thing that brings her to realize what it is she does want: [Mr. Darcy]. Also, set up the final scene with [Mr. Wickham].

The Scene: [Mr. Collins] shares the "truth" behind [Mr. Wickham's] behavior as well as what [Mr. Darcy] did to protect the MC from this bad guy: did [Mr. Darcy] threaten him? Pay him off? Call the police?

In this scene, [Mr. Collins] (already something the MC does not want) can be helpful (i.e., he is trying to redeem himself as well) _or_ malicious (he wants to hurt the MC because she doesn't like him). He is just here to contrast what the MC doesn't want with what she does.

Day 26

Austen: Elizabeth receives a letter from Mr. Darcy explaining his past actions and motives, causing her to reassess her opinions of him.

To Do: Bring the MC and [Mr. Darcy] together. [Mr. Darcy] needs to explain his motivations. They both fully acknowledge their misunderstandings and confess their feelings for each other.

The Scene: In this scene (Austen used a letter but unless you're writing a period piece, that likely won't work here), [Mr. Darcy] has to have the opportunity to sit the MC down and explain the details of a) his involvement in why [Mr. Bingley] and the MC did not work out (i.e. from Day 6, when he stopped her from "bothering" Mr. Bingley it was because he knew Mr. Bingley was with another woman in the office and didn't want the MC to see that and be humiliated) and b) the real truth about the relationship he has with [Mr. Wickham] - possibly he did commit crimes with [Mr. Wickham] in his youth, but only because his mother was dying and he needed to support her.

Day 27

Austen: Mr. Darcy proposes to Elizabeth again, and she accepts.

To Do: In the original, the plot threads included: Elizabeth and Mr. Darcy, the Bennet family's financial situation, Jane and Bingley, and Lydia and Wickham, the resolution of Mrs. Bennet's ambitions, and social tensions (i.e., class). First, focus on this primary thread of the MC and [Mr. Darcy] (but keep in mind the others also need completing, so if you can weave more than one in here too, that works).

The Scene: This is the scene where you close the final chapter of the key romantic story (the other threads can start being wrapped up here, or on Day 28, but the main romance should resolve today). Write the scene where they realize they have found true love and show a glimpse of what their future looks like - do they buy a cozy home, do they travel, do they have children. (Or, you can have the ending not be happily ever after: perhaps one goes to prison for his/her role in the crimes committed with [Mr. Wickham]).

Day 28

Austen: The novel ends with the various characters reflecting on the events that have transpired and looking forward to the future.

To Do: Wrap up all the threads. In the original this included: Elizabeth and Mr. Darcy (already resolved on Day 27), the Bennet family's financial situation, Jane and Bingley, and Lydia and Wickham. It also included the resolution of Mrs. Bennet's ambitions and social tensions (i.e., social class).

The Scene: Your threads will be different, but each of them need to be resolved. For each thread (and this final day could be more than one chapter), write the scene where they are resolved: i.e., show [Mr. Bingley's] life (did he get that big promotion, did he find love, did they have several children and their dream home).

Also, the resolution of whatever "baggage" (drive to get a good job, money, rebuild her relationship with her family) the MC carried with her through the story needs to be shown in this finale.

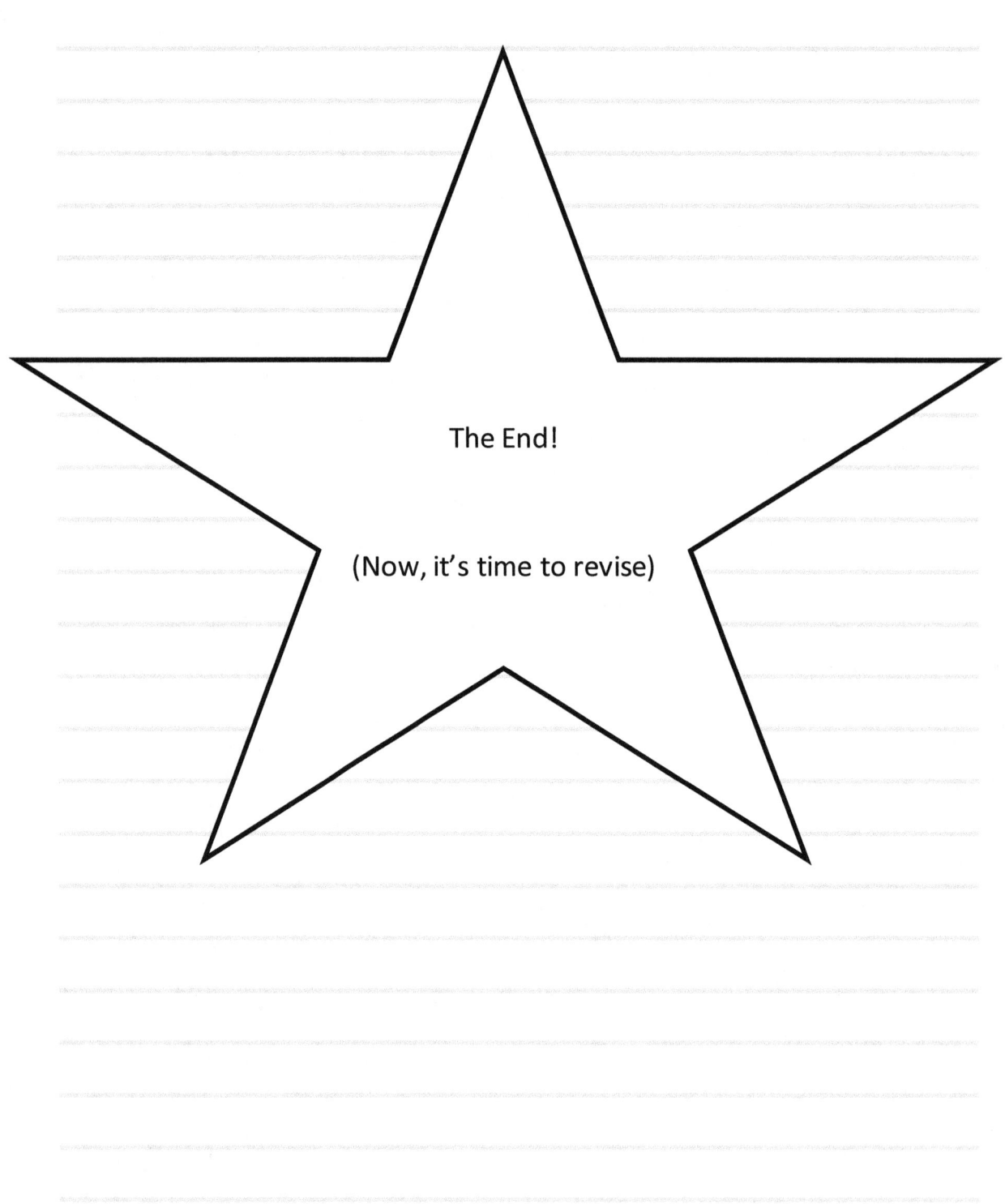

The End!

(Now, it's time to revise)

www.ingramcontent.com/pod-product-compliance
Lightning Source LLC
Chambersburg PA
CBHW080956120626
46546CB00010B/2916